Who's Jerry?

By
T. M. Jackson

Dedication

To my mother Robertina whose battle with mental illness,
did not impede her from instilling in me a lifetime love of learning.
To my sisters Roxanne and Toni who did their best to raise a
despondent impetuous child.
I thank you, I love you, and I hope you are
proud of the person I've become.

Scrubs Like Us For Us, 2020

Copyright © 2020 by T. M. Jackson

The publisher and author have no responsibility for the persistence or accuracy of URLs for external or third-party Internet Websites referred to in this publication and does not guarantee that any content on such Websites is, or will remain, accurate or appropriate.

The publisher, author, and the book are not associated with any product or vendor mentioned in this book. None of the companies referenced within the book have endorsed the book.

First paperback edition November 2020

Illustrations by Darwin Marfil

ISBN 978-1-7361282-2-0 (hardcover)
ISBN 978-1-7361282-1-3 (paperback)
ISBN 978-1-7361282-0-6 (ebook)

www.learnwithimani.com

Who's Jerry?

T. M. Jackson

Imani skipped through the front door.
"Guess what, Mommy!" she called. "I got an A on my
math test today."

Imani waited for an answer, but there was none.

"Mommy?" she said, walking toward the couch.
"You look funny. Do you want a hug?"

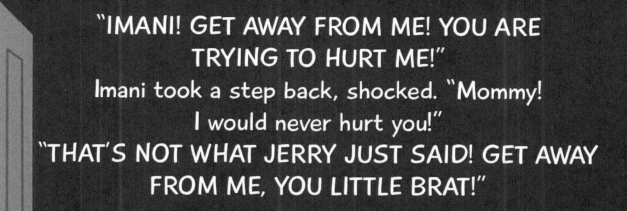

"IMANI! GET AWAY FROM ME! YOU ARE TRYING TO HURT ME!"
Imani took a step back, shocked. "Mommy! I would never hurt you!"
"THAT'S NOT WHAT JERRY JUST SAID! GET AWAY FROM ME, YOU LITTLE BRAT!"

Crying, Imani ran to her room. Mommy had been talking about her friend Jerry for weeks,
but Imani had never seen him. It was as if he was only in Mommy's mind.

But if that was true,
why did he hate Imani so much? What had she
done wrong?

The next morning, Imani fixed her own hair.
I really miss Mommy doing this for me, she thought.

As she made her own breakfast, she realized Mommy might be hungry, too.

"I'm going to school now, Mommy! Love you bunches! Rest up. I'll see you later!"

Imani was almost to the bus stop when Mommy ran out the door.

"IMANI! YOU FORGOT TO WEAR THIS! JERRY SAID IT WILL PROTECT YOU FROM THE MONSTERS ON THE BUS!"

Mommy put a pot on her head and ran back home. Imani tried to hide the pot, but she couldn't hide from the whispers on the bus.

"Why does she look dirty?"

"Why isn't her hair combed?"

"What's wrong with her?"

All morning, Imani was distracted. During her spelling test, she missed six easy words. During math, she added instead of subtracting. By recess, all she could think about was Mommy.

I don't understand what's wrong
with Mommy.
Why is she being so mean?
Why doesn't she love me
anymore?

"Hi Imani," a voice said.

"Hi, Mr. Jackson."
"You've been looking sad lately, and you got a C
on your spelling and math tests
today," Mr. Jackson said. "That's not like you.
Are you okay?"

Imani shook her head.
"Would you like me to call your
mom?"

"No!"

"Is your Dad back from his work trip?"

Imani sniffled. Then, slowly, she nodded. "Okay, let's call him instead."

Imani listened as Mr. Jackson told her dad that she'd been having a bad day. "I think she needs her dad," he said.

When school ended, Imani saw Daddy waiting for her outside.

"What's going on, Imani? Why do you look so messy?"
Imani was quiet.
"Imani," Daddy said again. "What's wrong?"

Nervous, Imani blurted out, "Daddy, Mommy hates me. She doesn't talk to me or help me get ready for school anymore. And her friend Jerry keeps telling her that I'm going to hurt her."

"Who's Jerry?"

"I think he's her invisible friend, Daddy," Imani whispered.

At home, Daddy brought Imani inside. All the lights were off, but they could see Mommy sitting on the bed.

"Nandi, what is going on here?" Daddy asked. "What's wrong with you?"

Mommy just stared at the wall.

Daddy tried again. "Nandi, who is Jerry?"
Mommy still didn't speak.

"Has she been like this the whole time I was gone?"
Daddy asked Imani.

"She's been acting weird for a while, Daddy.
She was hiding Jerry from everyone before, but now she
doesn't anymore," Imani said.

Daddy leaned down. "Imani, I think your mommy needs to
see a doctor. Can you call your auntie and ask her to meet
us at the hospital?"

Auntie waited with me while Daddy talked to the doctor. After what felt like forever, he came out.

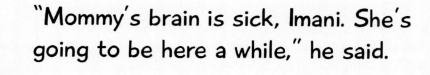

"Mommy's brain is sick, Imani. She's going to be here a while," he said.

"Sick?" Imani cried out, "is she going to be okay?"

"Yes," Daddy said. "The doctors are going to fix her up for you. Till then, baby, you're going to stay with me."

Imani missed Mommy . . .

. . . but she liked Daddy
teaching her how to fix
things . . .

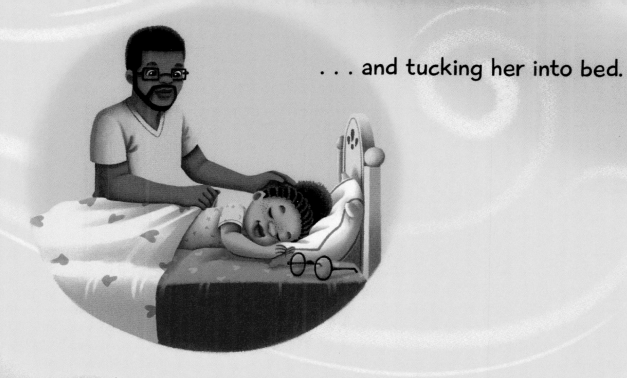

. . . and tucking her into bed.

Then, finally, Daddy told Imani that Mommy was coming home!

"Imani, I missed you so much!
I'm sorry for how I acted.
Jerry is gone now, and he won't be back."

"Really, Mommy? Does that mean your brain isn't sick anymore?"

"It means as long as I take my medicine, everything will be okay. You see, I have something called schizophrenia.
"SKIP SO WHAT EAT A?"

"It's pronounced skit-suh-freh-nee-uh," Mommy said.

"It made me act weird and see and hear things that aren't real, like Jerry. I thought Jerry was trying to help me, so I did what he said to do. I love you bunches, and I'm so sorry I was mean to you.

"We are all going to help your mom stay healthy," Daddy said. "Aunt Nichelle is coming to live with you, and I'm moving closer to help you and Mommy. How does that sound?"

"Cool!" Imani said.

"Now, let's go home!" Mommy said. "I miss doing my baby's hair!"

"Mommy's back and she still loves me."

Resources

It takes a village to change the stigma of mental health in our communities. Please use the following links as resources for your continued mental growth and well-being.

Black Girls Smile - https://www.blackgirlssmile.org/

Black Mental Health Alliance - https://blackmentalhealth.com/

Boris Lawrence Henson Foundation - https://borislhensonfoundation.org/

Black Emotional and Mental Health Collective - https://www.beam.community/

National Alliance on Mental Illness - https://www.nami.org/Home

Loveland Foundation - https://thelovelandfoundation.org/

Eustress, Inc - https://www.eustressinc.org/

The Steve Fund - https://www.stevefund.org/

Lee Thompson Young Foundation - https://www.ltyfoundation.org/

National Latino Behavioral Health Association - http://www.nlbha.org/

Therapy for Latinx - https://www.therapyforlatinx.com/

One Sky Center - http://www.oneskycenter.org/

We are Native - https://www.wernative.org/

National Asian American Pacific Islander Mental Health Association - https://www.naapimha.org/

Asian Mental Health Collective - https://www.asianmhc.org/

Arab-American Family Support Center - https://www.aafscny.org/ Khalil Center - https://khalilcenter.com/